CN00651846

Stonehenge

INTRODUCTION.

THE lack of any thoroughly accurate survey of Stonehenge will be a sufficient reason for the production of the present plan, in addition to those already published. Neither the plans of Wood, Smith, Colt Hoare, Sir Henry James, nor Hawkshaw, lay any claim apparently to accuracy greater than a few inches, thus missing important results and deductions; whereas that now produced is correct to a few tenths of an inch, in fact quite as closely as the surface of the stone can be estimated in most cases.

Though on a small scale for convenience of use, the accuracy of this plan is as great as that of a sheet of ordinary delicacy about 4 or 5 feet across. The original measurements of the stone circle, on the triangulation lines, and the well-wrought stones, were taken to the nearest $\frac{1}{10}$ of an inch, and in all cases correct to within $\frac{1}{4}$ inch; the plotting and copying (on double the scale now lithographed) were correspondingly done to about a thousandth of an inch, in many parts with a magnifier: the present photolithograph is therefore intentionally accurate to $\frac{1}{2000}$ of an inch; and, considering the various sources of error, it may be usefully examined, and measurements taken from it, to $\frac{1}{500}$ or $\frac{1}{1000}$ of an inch. Those readers who merely wish for approximate ideas, can use this for general inspection like any rougher plan; but for investigations on the arrangement and exact dimensions of any part, this plan, measured with an accurate plotting scale and magnifier, will probably give results as trustworthy as could be obtained on the ground.

The work was begun in 1874, but after going some way with it, it was abandoned owing to the errors of the ordinary surveying chain used. In 1877 I made a new pattern of chain, expressly for accurate work;* and with this the present survey was made, in June and September of that year. It was laid by, partly owing to being engaged with plans of the other remains in the southern counties, and partly waiting to obtain accurate sunrise observations at midsummer.

* The essentials of this pattern are, 1st, rhomboidal eyes; 2nd, long links of 20 inches; 3rd, no intermediate rings; 4th, dividing marks on the middles of the links, fixed (from the official standard) after the chain is made and strained; 5th, numbering marks on every link; 6th, lightness, for stretching without perceptible error over hollows.

B 2

The theoretical considerations of the date and origin of this structure are necessarily entered on here, as many of the details now brought to light bear strongly on those questions; but the object of this publication is more to state facts than theories.

In order to give a fair impression, all the considerations of importance have been mentioned, on each side of the argument, that could be found by careful reading and personal reference; and as my own opinion has fluctuated more than once, I may at least hope to have attained thorough impartiality.

The various sections are divided as follows :—

FACTS.

1. DESCRIPTION OF THE PLANS.
2. DETAILS OF THE STONES.
3. METHODS OF WORKMANSHIP.
4. NUMBER OF STONES.

THEORIES.

5. THE WORK NOT COMPLETE.
6. POSITION OF THE "ALTAR STONE."
7. MIDSUMMER SUNRISE.
8. SEQUENCE SHOWN BY CONSTRUCTION.
9. SEQUENCE SHOWN BY MEASURES.
10. OBJECTS FOUND.
11. SUMMARY OF EVIDENCES ON PRE-ROMAN AGE.
12. SUMMARY OF EVIDENCES ON POST-ROMAN AGE.
13. SUMMARY OF EVIDENCES ON THE USE.
14. CONCLUDING REMARKS.

STONEHENGE.

1. Description of the Plans.

BESIDE the explanation given on the plans, some general arrangements require notice, before mentioning the stones in detail. Offsets were taken to fix the various points, but their estimated rectangularity was never trusted beyond a few inches, all long lines being tied in by triangulation. The arrows projecting from the stones, show the extent to which the top of each stone has shifted by leaning; this was estimated by considering both faces of the stones, but owing to their often tapering, the extremity of the arrow does not necessarily show the place of the top of the face. It may be reckoned that the ground-level outline of the stone, shown on the plan, has moved about $\frac{1}{10}$ of the shift of the top. The thinner outline of the form above the ground, is only given when the stone is more regular above than below; as its position was arranged probably with reference to its most regular part. The more regular part is always the most prominent (except on the back of No. 52), as the stone was shaped at its largest part. The character of the shading, &c., is sufficiently explained on the plan. The five stones "standing in 1747" are from Wood's plan; and as they are overthrown, or much shifted since his time, it seemed desirable to make this plan as complete as possible by inserting them. They were plotted from Wood's measurements, in connection with neighbouring stones still unshifted, and then adjusted by means of the latter on this plan. Of course their positions and their outlines are far less accurate than those of the other stones, but they are nevertheless the best now to be had; and their present positions are also shown in unshaded dotted outline. No distinction is made on this plan between perfect stones and mere stumps of which the upper part is removed (though these are detailed in the description), as for considerations of arrangement this is wholly immaterial—unlike the shift, which is important.

The large circle is the mean circle which agrees best to all the sarsen stones,* making

* These are tertiary sandstones left lying on the chalk after the denudation of those beds. The bluestones are from Cornwall or Ireland.

allowance for their shiftings. The next circle similarly is fitted to the outer bluestones; though to what point of them it should agree is not certain, as their inner faces are often convex, unlike the sarsens; whether the innermost curve, or the inner corners of the stone, or something between, is not clear. The trilithons* are not on a circle, and the scheme of their placing is obscure. The innermost semicircle is fitted to the bluestones, like the others. The centres of these three circles, and of the outer earth circle, are shown surrounded by little rings on the plan; the radii of these little rings are equal in each case to the mean error of the various points of the respective circles from a true figure. This mean error of the inner bluestones is $1 \cdot 7$ inch; of the outer bluestones, 8 inches; of the sarsen circle, $3 \cdot 2$ inches; and of the earth circle (shown in Plate II.), 10 inches. The two fine lines crossing obliquely near the centre, will be seen to be in line with four short pieces on the outskirts of the plan, numbered 91, 92, 93, and 94. These are the lines connecting the centres of the stones (91 and 93), and of the pits or barrows (92 and 94), shown in Plate II., lying on the outer earth circle. They so nearly intersect the centre, that it is important to show them on this delicate plan; their probable error is about $\pm$ 2 inches $= \frac{1}{100}$ inch on the plan.

The mean axis was determined by (1) the middle of the entrance, which is closely the same at all heights of the stones, though the opening widens 20 inches at the top; (2) the centre of the main circle; (3) the estimated original place of the great trilithon stones 55 and 56, considering that they have slewed northwards in falling; the estimated distance between them, eliminating the slew, is 13 inches, and this (though quite independent) closely agrees with the standing trilithons which are $12 \cdot 8$ and $12 \cdot 4$ inches; (4) half the average spacing between the stones, allowed from the side of No. 16; this is very vague, as the interval varies from 26 to 51 inches; the mean, being 36, gives 18 for the half-distance.

The mean axis drawn differs from these elements as follows:—

	Axis.
Exactly through	entrance opening.
	$\cdot 6$ inch from sarsen circle centre.
From estimated centre of trilithon, $\cdot 4$ inch	
Approximately by No. 16, $1 \cdot 8$,,	

---

* This term is here restricted to the five internal groups, of two uprights and one impost each, and not applied to the circle stones, as by some writers.

The very close agreement of the elements is remarkable, but each was determined before they were compared.

Outside the circle will be seen five crosses on each side of the plan, beside others in the circle; these are exactly 25 feet or 300 inches apart; they may be considered the corners of squares of 25 feet (or a large square of 100 feet quartered in each direction), drawn on the mean axis as a basis, the sides being omitted to avoid confusion. The object is to give a scale extending over every part of the plan, so that distortion in photolithographing, and irregular contraction of the paper, may be eliminated for accurate measurements; a scale drawn at the edge in the usual way, is peculiarly liable to derangement; and for rough purposes any inch measure will do, as the plan is on the simple scale of $\frac{1}{100}$.

It should be remembered in comparing this plan with others, or with accurate measurements, that some inches difference may easily occur if the stones be not measured on the same level as here; in all cases the most perfect part of the stone was taken close to the ground, and if it had a better form above, this is also shown.

To Wood's plan (1747), Smith (in 1770) added Nos. 39, 72, and 160 a; Colt Hoare adds No. 71; Hawkshaw adds a piece which I could not see, between 14 and 36; and finally I may add 66, which makes its first appearance in this plan.

The second plan is not of such accuracy as the first; the stones are only approximately reduced, within about $\frac{1}{100}$ inch; and the earth circle may perhaps in parts have some errors as large. Its mean error already stated (10 inches) was determined by a large scale plan. A true circle is here drawn, with short breaks at each measured point, such points being shown by a small cross, more or less in or out of the true line; thus enabling the differences to be easily seen. The distance of the outer ditch and bank was measured in four places, also marked on the plan. The levels of them, taking the area levels as o, are thus :—

Top of bank .. .. $+ 9$ to 18 variation, $+ 14$ mean

Bottom of ditch .. $- 16$ to 39 „ $- 27$. „ $= $ rise 41 $\Big]$ from bottom

$= $ rise 17 $\Big]$ of ditch.

Top of faint outer bank $- 16$ to $+ 1$ „ $- 10$ „

The levels of the various parts of the area are marked in inches and tenths, above the Ordnance bench-mark on the Friar's Heel, No. 96.

The method of marking banks and ditches, &c., has been adopted, after much con-

sideration and experiment, as being free from the ambiguity of ordinary shading, and also admitting of greater precision of drawing.

The two mounds within the area are shown on this plan; they have been often called pits (from Wood), owing to their having a hole in the top, probably from old diggings in them. The northern one is nearly half cut away by a road; it has a ditch and bank, unlike the other. The forms of all the outlying stones, Nos. 91, 93, 95, and 96, are given in the corner of Plate I.; the closer shade on 91 showing approximately the place of the base, before it tipped outward.

The details of the junction of the circle and the avenue, and of the banks that cross the avenue lower down, are all carefully entered, exactly as they appear on the ground.

The avenue is raised between the banks, which are very faint on their inner edges, and in all parts flat and ill-defined. The north-east end and the branches are very faint, and scarcely traceable in parts. The greater width of the north branch is curious, and as it is not noticed in the small plans of the Ordnance Survey and Hoare, there would almost seem to be some uncertainty in the plan, as it has not been verified; three measured points on each side however agree.

The parallel banks are quite unnoticed in Hoare's and the Ordnance plans. They are slight but sharp, and the ground between them has been lowered. Of what date they may be is not certain, but if not intended for a recent road they are probably ancient. Against the idea of a road there are the following facts: (1) They are 42 feet apart, but the road they would join is the usual regulation width of 30 feet; (2) there is no ditch, and the ground is flat between; whereas the main requisite of a road is to raise the centre, and make side ditches; (3) they end abruptly, and have been recommenced farther easterly (traceable by lines of buttercups, though now ploughed), and also westerly as seen on the small plan of $\frac{1}{10000}$ on Plate II.; this discontinuous work is not like modern road making; (4) the western part passes a barrow; and here, instead of cutting a slice out of it to make room for a road, the bank runs up over the foot of the barrow, and the barrow ditch is flattened at its edges but not filled up; also the barrow is just in the midst of the length of this piece. All these points are unlike the beginning of a modern road. The banks pass over the avenue west bank and ditch, but are cut away at the east bank sharply, to allow of a cart track passing, which runs down the avenue bank. This looks as if they were older than the cart track, and therefore not recent.

The row of barrows on the $\frac{1}{10000}$ plan are very nearly in a straight line, except the last. Their average departure of their centres is 52 inches, on a line 850 feet long in all. Further details of their distances are given in 9. *Sequence shown by Measures.*

---

2. Details of the Stones.

After much consideration, the irregular lettering and numbering of Colt Hoare was abandoned; it begins with the entrance stones as A¹ and A², goes then to the trilithons B¹ B² . . . F¹ F², thus not leaving enough letters for the outer circle without a double alphabet, and then using numbers for the bluestones. The present system is entirely by numbers for each stone; lettering the fragments of a single stone; as 59 a, 59 b, 59 c. The order begins always at the axis, and goes with positive rotation E., S., W., N. 1 to 30 are the outer sarsens (allowing numbers for the blank spaces); 31 to 49 the outer bluestones; 51 to 60 the trilithons; 61 to 72 the inner bluestones; 80 the "altar stone"; 91 to 96 the outlying stones and tumuli; the lintels are all numbered 100 more than their higher numbered supporter; i.e. the numbers agreeing with 1 prefixed to the lintel. Thus the numbering of the sarsens begins at 1 and 51, and the bluestones at 31 and 61; an easily remembered arrangement. The numbers of the successive circles are all in sequence, though each set begins a fresh decade; except that No. 50 is unapplied, but as a lintel in that set has no supporter it appropriates No. 150 very suitably.

The following details of the stones are accompanied by Hoare's lettering for reference. The levels are in inches above the Ordnance bench-mark on the Friar's Heel, No. 96. The heights are above the ground at the spot in question. The word "Outline" is reserved for fallen stones; "Plan" for the horizontal section of stones. "Emergence" is the line of the face at ground-level. "Impost" is used for a trilithon top-stone; "Lintel" for a circle top-stone.

No. Sarsens.	Hoare.	Height.	Level of top.	Diff. from mean of group (213·3).	REMARKS.
1	A¹	159	208·1	− 5·2	
2		170	211·9	− 1·4	
3		171	209·3	− 4·0	
4		170	211·9	− 1·4	

c

No. Sarsens.	Hoare.	Height.	Level of top.	Diff. from mean of group (213.3).	REMARKS.
5		174	215.0	+ 1.7	
6		165	215.9	+ 2.6	
7		162	211.3	− 2.0	
8		..	..	..	Sides worked.
9 a, b		..	..	..	9 b, sides worked; end very flat, with tenon.
10		160	220.0	+ 6.7	
11		96	..	..	
12		..	..	..	Two tenons on end.
14*		..	..	..	31 to 36 thick.
15		..	..	..	Two tenons on end.
16		165	215.5	+ 2.2	Bench-mark at 78.3 level.
19		..	..	..	End and north side worked. Top 13 out of ground.
21		152	212.7	− .6	
22		153	209.2	− 4.1	
23		153	209.4	− 3.9	
25		..	..	..	Fallen westwards.
26		..	..	..	No worked faces.
27		167	214.2	+ .9	
28		165	214.4	+ 1.1	
29		156	212.3	− 1.0	
30	A'	153	207.6	− 5.7	
Bluestones.					
31	1	..	127.5	..	Rounded top, broken.
32	3	..	..	..	Foot buried, fixed by probing; two faces shown here on top. 17.5 thick, all down.
33	4	..	..	..	
34	5	38	..	..	Upright.
35 a, b	6, n n	..	..	..	Only a stump, widely cracked, like two stones. 35 b, probably part of 35 a.
36	7	..	..	..	North end buried; a square stone lying with edge up, emerging at lines drawn across face.
37	8	..	..	..	} Schistose, see 14, shaded plans from Wood, 1747.
39	10	..	..	..	
40	11	..	..	..	Overthrown before 1747.

* 14 was leaning on 38 in 1747 emerging at the full line; it now has fallen farther, occupying the dotted outline, and resting on 38, at a slope of 1 in 4. 38 has apparently tipped over sideways, as well as inwards, owing to the pressure of 14 upon its east corner; having been in 1747 in the shaded plan, and now emerging at the dotted line (which also shows place of east end under turf), rising 45° to north. 39 occupied the shaded plan on end in 1747, but has been pushed inwards to the present dotted outline by the fall of 14, and now rises 1 in 2 to north.

No. Bluestones.	Hoare.	Height.	Level of top.	Diff. from mean of group.	REMARKS.
41	12	..	..	..	No flat faces. Small cross at estimated original site of centre.
42	13	..	..	..	Fallen in 1747, before trilithon fell.
43	14	..	..	..	On edge. Rises 50° to east.
44	15	..	..	..	Small cross as above, but shifted altogether (?).
45	16	..	..	..	„ „ „ . Flat sides and top.
46	17	..	..	..	Hornstone.
47	18	..	..	..	Leaning in, outline of top shown.
48	19	..	..	..	Hornstone as 46.
49	20	..	132·9	..	Broken, rounded at top.
Sarsens.					
51	B¹	201	252·4	..	
52	B²	..	255·7	..	
53	C¹ ⎫	212	265·2	..	
54	C² ⎭				
55 a, b, D¹		..	..	..	At south end a large projecting foot left in working, to go under ground. Concave on inner face.
56	D²	..	..	..	The leaning stone. The shaded part south of it shows how far back (at the least) it must have been when upright. This trilithon upset by the Duke of Buckingham digging in 1620.
57	E¹	..	..	.. ⎫	This trilithon fell 3rd January, 1797. Shaded plans from Wood, 1747. Dotted outlines show the present places.
58	E²	..	..	.. ⎭	
59 a,b,c F¹		..	..	..	Fallen before 1575; see view in Camden.
60	F²	198	247·8	..	
Bluestones.			Mean 148·8.		
61	21	..	125·0	..	Broken top.
62	22	..	143·0	− 5·8	
63	23	..	147·0	− 1·8	
64	24	..	..	..	Only a stump, 3 inches high.
65	25	..	..	..	Broken near ground.
66	omitted	..	..	..	Only a stump.
67	27	..	..	..	Larger stone, different in style to others.
68	26	..	153·1	+ 4·3	Worked groove down north side. Supports 56.
69	28	..	157·0	+ 8·2	
70	29	..	144·1	− 4·7	Tipped out by foot of 58 in falling. Shaded plan Wood's, dotted outline present place. Wood is wrong in shape.
71	30	..	..	..	
72	31	..	..	..	

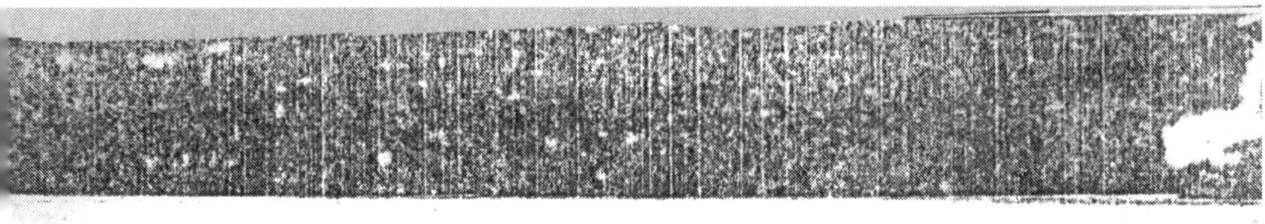

No. Bluestones.	Hoare.	Height.	Level of top.	Diff. from mean of group.	Remarks.
80	Altarstone	..	mid 60·0	..	Rises east, at a slope = 7·3 on whole length.
91	..	..	..	..	This leans outward; the outline is shown in Plate II. No working.
92	..	..	..	..	Mound with central pit.
93	..	..	..	..	Upright stone. A patch on each side, and on outer face, wrought.
94	..	..	..	..	Mound with central pit, ditch and ridge around. Half cut away by road.
95	..	..	..	..	Lying quite flat, upper face at ground level. Wrought end and sides.
96	Friar's heel	..	..	..	Leaning west, unwrought.
101	..	..	top 237·6	..	Across entrance. } Not shown on ground plan.
102	..	..	237·3	.. }	Lintels *in situ*. } Not shown on ground plan.
105	..	..	241·6	.. }	Lintels *in situ*. } Not shown on ground plan.
107	..	..	239·9	.. }	Lintels *in situ*. } Not shown on ground plan.
120	..	..	..	..	Portion of lintel, top 16 inches out of ground.
122	..	..	239·5	..	*In situ*, not on ground plan.
127	..	..	..	..	Sides worked, ends broken.
130	..	..	240·5	..	*In situ*, not on plan.
150	..	..	..	..	Bluestone impost, unsuited for any existing pair.
152	..	{mid underside}	252·7	..	252·2 at north end. } *In situ*, not on plan.
154	..	„	265·2	..	} *In situ*, not on plan.
156	D^2	..	..	..	Lintel overthrown 1620. Marks on it cut in 1827 or 8.
158	E^2	..	..	..	Lintel fell in 1797.
160 *a,b,c*	F^2	..	..	..	Fragments of lintel. No trace of mortises on upper sides.

The original height of the fallen trilithons 55–58 out of the ground was carefully estimated; all together they are as follows:—

	inches.	inches.
Nos. 51, 52	201, top of upright;	241, top of impost.
53, 54	212 „	256 „
55, 56	263 ± 2 „	288 ± 2 „
57, 58	214 ± 3 „	258? „
59, 60	198 „	238? „

The dimensions of the imposts, and trilithon tops, &c., vary so irregularly that they do not seem worth detailing. The average dimensions are, with the mean of the differences from the average,

	inches.		inches.	
Trilithon tops ..	73·2 long,	2·5 mean difference;	39·7 wide,	3·9 mean difference.
Imposts	184·2 „	2·6 „	48·0 (at ends)	2·7 „
Circle stones tops ..	67·1 „	5·0 „	31·5	6·0 „
Lintels	133·7 „	2·8 „	41·0	3·0 „
Tenons apart ..	34·3	5·0 „		

.The ground levels are marked on Plate II., like the preceding, in inches above the bench-mark on the Heel stone, 96.

The circle of the tops of the sarsens has apparently a tilt, according to the levels, averaging at the maximum 4 inches above and below the mean level; the nodes of the plane being at No. 5, and opposite, and the highest point between 27 and 28. The assumption of this tilt reduces the mean error from a true plane, from 2·75 to 1·9 inches (or as 10 : 7); it is most likely that they would not be placed in exactly a level plane, and the tilt of 4 inches = 24'. The mean level of the circle tops, 213·3 above datum, is not the mean of existing stones (212·4), as their irregular distribution would affect it; but it is the mean of the 4 mean levels of the 4 quadrants.

Whether the stones were arranged by their inner or outer faces, is settled by the fact that the inner faces fit a mean circle, with just half the amount of error of the outer faces: observe Nos. 1, 2, 3, and 21, 22, and 23. Also the flattest sides are placed in, very plainly seen on the ground in 3, 28, 29, and specially 2 and 60. 52 and 54, though better on the back above, have the best side of the base placed inwards.

The azimuths of the principal lines are as follows:—

Mean axis of circle as drawn	30' ± 2'
Mean axis of avenue..	18'
Middle of avenue from middle of entrance	15'
Axis symmetrical with 91, 93, 92, 94 ..	0' (adopted as arbitrary datum).

The avenue axis apparently runs to 14 inches north-west of the middle of the entrance; but the banks are so very vague, and so much damaged near the circle, that this is not very certain; perhaps ± 5 inches.*

3. Methods of Workmanship.

Nearly all of the stones have had more or less dressing; some dressed all over, others only on prominent parts; so as to give a regular figure at the end or edges, with faulty parts elsewhere. The method of cleaving the stone is shown by the large flat stone 95, one corner of which has been begun to be cut off; a row of 6 holes, 1½ inch long, ¾ wide, 1 and 1¼ deep, and averaging 6 inches apart (varying from 4 to 8), are sunk in nearly a straight

---

* This sign ± is used throughout to denote "probable error"; i.e. the truth is as likely to be within 5 inches on either side of the statement, as to be over 5 inches from it : *vide* De Morgan, Airy, Merriman &c.

line; they are sloping sided, as would be made by irregular tools. There are no traces of such cleaving holes on the edges of any of the other stones, apparently owing to their subsequent dressing. Large quantities were cut away in surface work; the projecting foot left on 55 shows about 15 inches of stone to have been cut away all across the face of the block. The method of cutting down a face was by running large shallow grooves across the stone, probably cutting away the intervening ridges in making the next series of grooves; these wide grooves were then apparently removed by running narrower ones across them. The wide ones are finely shown on the back of 59, one 17 wide and $2\frac{1}{2}$ deep, with a sharp ridge on either side, and with three faint cross grooves. On the side of 59 next to 60 there are small grooves, 6 in a width of 22 inches, the best of them 48 long, all very flat. No grooving is left on 55, though so much has been cut out. The back of 54 has 3 large vertical grooves, 50, 20, and 28 wide; also slight cross grooves, 4 in a width of 39 inches. On the back of 52 there are two faint horizontal grooves in 11 inches wide; also one slight horizontal ridge left on the flat inner face of 51. The only grooving on the bluestones is on 67; a slight vertical groove 14 wide, and 2 or 3 horizontal ones at 2 or 3 inches apart: this stone is a very dissimilar shape to the others, being wide, flat, and thickest at the top.

The tenons have been worked to an irregular mammiform shape; those fallen are much damaged, and have nearly disappeared in some cases; but the finest for examination is on the top of 60, reached by a ladder, being 17 feet from the ground. Here the general surface is very flat, all carefully picked; and though showing the picking, yet apparently a true plane within the depth of the pickmarks. A ridge runs along the outer, north-west, side, 3 inches high, and a slight ridge on south-west. The tenon is $15\frac{1}{2}$ inches wide at base, and 7 inches high. There is a similar sort of tray shape, with a raised edge $2\frac{1}{2}$ inches high, on the top of 51; the impost (still *in situ*) having a corresponding sinking around its edge to fit the ledge on the edge of the upright. The top of 52 is similarly cut, with a ledge 1 inch high, and dressed very smooth and regular. This is seen as they are not erected with the tops quite parallel, 51 sloping down 1·2 inches to 52, on the 77 inches of its top width, thus leaving a gap.

The trilithon imposts are cut 5 and 6 inches wider at the top than the under side; and are flat on the inner, and convex on the outer side.

Whether the mortise holes were cut to fit the distance of the tenons, after erecting the stones, or whether the work was first planned and the stones erected to fit the

mortises, is not clear in the outer circle; probably the latter, as there is a ridge $1\frac{1}{2}$ inch high across the top of 30, rising between the lintel blocks. The lintel 101 has a projecting tongue at the middle of each end, keying into a corresponding vertical groove in the adjacent block; 130 has the corresponding groove on the end joining 101, and a tongue on the other end; the next lintel with corresponding groove is lost. 102 is similar, with a groove for the tongue of 101, and a tongue on the other end. 122 has a tongue on each end, which projects about 3 inches like the others. 130 has a curious mistake in it, of a third mortise hole, too large, and too near its middle.

----

4. Number of Stones.

The decimal numbers of many stone circles is worth notice, in connection with Stonehenge. The outer circle of sarsens has 30 stones (or places); the trilithons are 10 stones; and the bluestones are probably incomplete. Similarly the circle at Winterbourne Abbas, Dorset, has 10 stones (one missing); the circles of Dawnsmaen, Boscawenoon, and Kenidjack, in the Land's End, are each of 20 stones; and though the latter have also some missing, and it might be questioned whether a gap was not left intentionally, yet it does not affect the point that the circle is divided into a decimal number of places, though each may not contain a stone. The trouble of dividing decimally, instead of continued halving into 8, 16, or 32, or taking $\frac{1}{6}$ by the radius, shows that importance was attached to it, especially as it is so frequent. Other cases, where the circle is less perfect, are less decisive; but the three circles of the Hurlers near St. Cleer are credited with having had 29, 29, and 27 stones, which may very possibly have been 30 originally. In Cumberland, the Eskdale circle was of 40 or 41 stones, the Swinside circle of 60 stones, and the Gunnerskeld circle, Westmoreland, 29 + or − 1 stones, or spaces for stones, which show apparently the same decimal division.

----

5. The Work not complete.

Though it is certain that some stones have been removed, this fact does not account for the whole case. First, the evidence for the stones being removed. Inigo Jones says that some bluestones were taken away since he first saw them. The Earl of Pembroke told

Aubrey that an altar stone was found in the middle of the area, and carried away to St. James's [*]; there is, however, no such stone in Inigo Jones's plan, nor is there any hole or sharp sinking of the earth in the middle of the area, such as would be left by abstracting a large stone sunken in the ground. No stones are missing since Wood's plan in 1747. There are several stones that have been overthrown and broken, and of which only portions remain, see Nos. 8, 15, 19, and 26; from each of these at least half the stone has been removed for certain. Also of four bluestones only stumps remain, Nos. 35, 64, 65, and 66; a further evidence of violence and of removal.

The evidence for non-completion of the outer sarsens, is in the very much smaller stone 11; this is only half the usual breadth, and 8 feet instead of 14 feet high like the others. At the same time, as it exactly occupies the proper place between 10 and 12, and (allowing for its tip out) fits the circle better than some others, we cannot deny the intention of its similarity. Again, Nos. 21 and 23 are both defective in size, compared with the rest; these show that 11 was no single freak, but was the result of not having better material. If then the builders ran so short as to have to use such a stone as 11, is it not very probable that they had not enough to finish the circle? Whether the site of Stonehenge was determined by a quantity of large sarsens occurring there, from the denudation of the beds above, or whether they were collected from far, is uncertain; there are few or none such large sarsens to be found now elsewhere. The absence of any blocks of waste stone, and of any smaller sarsens unsuitable for building, near the site, suggests that the blocks were collected from all parts, and trimmed before carriage; though the fitting of tenons, &c., might be done at the structure. Might any fragments be found at the groups of sarsens elsewhere, showing the remains of the cleavage holes? The chips of bluestone and sarsen together in the barrows, would seem to have been chipped off after erection; as we shall see that there is internal evidence that the bluestones are later than the sarsens.

The outer bluestones have been usually supposed to be the remains of a complete circle; there are at present 18 (perhaps 19); and the places seem to be 44, if they were equally arranged. Now a point apparently hitherto unnoticed in their positions is that 14 out of the 18 are in pairs opposite to one another (31, 34?, 36, and 43, being the only unpaired stones); and also that in the four 37 to 40, and in the four 46 to 49 which match them, there occur two stones in each set which are dissimilar to all the others,

[*] ? Berwick St. James, near Stonehenge.

being schistose or hornstone in place of syenite. If the circle ever were complete, it is highly improbable that the spoilers would remove stones always in pairs opposite to each other. The probability of 14 out of 18 stones being by chance opposite to each other in a set of 44 places is about 5000 to 1. The stone No. 44 is omitted in this consideration, as its original place is not quite certain; but if in the outer bluestones, it probably paired to 34, which would increase the improbability of casualty to over 30,000 to 1. Thus there is practical proof, from the arrangement, that there never were many more bluestones.

The celebrated bluestone impost 150 is another evidence of incompletion; for if ever erected, and then overthrown, the loose lintel would naturally be removed before the supporters. It will not fit any of the existing bluestones, as the mortises are (judging by the sarsen imposts) too close together for any now standing; and it cannot be intended for one of a set of continuous lintels, as its ends beyond the holes are too long. It is just adapted for a very close pair of bluestones, proportioned like the trilithons. The idea that some of the fallen bluestones may likewise be imposts, lying with the holes downwards, is unlikely when examined in detail; 36 has certainly been an upright, and the fallen ones 41 to 45 are mostly buried more or less at one end, and are all much more irregular than 150, 45 being the only one at all approaching its regularity of cutting. Hence 150 seems to be unique.

The flat stone 95 on the earth circle is another evidence of incompletion, as across one corner a row of holes is sunk for cleaving it (see large outline in corner of Plate I.), which have never been carried out. The sides and ends are trimmed, and the whole is as large as a trilithon upright; but it has no trace of tenons on the end, which is flat, smooth, and good. Its present position is a puzzle; the surface is very irregular on the upper face, which is, however, as nearly level, and also as nearly flush with the ground surface, as it can be estimated. The sides are now exposed, owing evidently to modern digging for examination of it. By its sunken position and absence of any dip it seems unlikely that it was in progress to another site, or that it was to be placed on end where it now lies, or that it has fallen. But it lies askew, in a manner unlike any other stone, except the "altar," No. 80, which makes it not look as if finally fixed. In lying to one side of the axis it resembles No. 96. Were these ever to be paired by others, forming narrow gateways in the avenue?

D

6. Position of the "Altar Stone."

With regard to the altar stone, its skew position, as in No. 95, is against its being now in its intended site; and for and against the theory of its having stood as the impost of a second trilithon, on the top of trilithon 55, 56, we may note : (1) Henry of Huntingdon's well-known description, which Hoare explains as referring to the trilithons seen over the circle lintels; (2) that it lies skew at present ; (3) that there are traces of what may be either natural hollows or shallow mortises for supporters on the top of the impost 154, at 18 to 30½ from north end and 26 to 38 from south end; the true mortise holes underneath being at 9 to 28½ from north end, and 24½ to 50½ from south end. But against the theory, (1) the altar is 198 long, though partly buried, and found by probing at the ends, the impost being only 184 long; and as none of the imposts overhang, it is unlikely that a super-impost would do so; (2) it lies nearly flat at present without more slope (7 inches on 200) than might easily be produced by the Duke of Buckingham's and Cunnington's diggings; (3) it is deeply sunk in the ground, and that regularly, and not on an edge which might dig in in falling; whereas the impost 158 is said in falling only to have struck 7 inches deep, even on its edge ; (4) it is unlikely that any person would or could displace it, if perched on the top of a trilithon 24 feet high; any other damage, such as digging down the trilithon altogether, would be easier done ; (5) and there are no supporters remaining for it.

7. Midsummer Sunrise.

The popular idea of the sun rising on the longest day behind the Friar's Heel, No. 96, was carefully tested by theodolite observations. When duly corrected for excentricities of theodolite and of signal, for minute change of declination between epochs of solstice and observation, and for altitude of horizon on rising slightly to the back of the circle, the azimuths are

	From middle entrance.	From behind middle trilithon.
Middle of avenue at parallel banks	15'	
True axis of avenue, 18'.		
Axis of circle, 30' ± 2'.		
North side of Friar's Heel	32'	11'
Peak „ „	1° 45'	1° 24'
South side „ „	2° 45'	2° 24'
Beginning of sunrise, midsummer 1880	1° 4'	1° 2'
Middle „ „	1° 30'	1° 28'
End „ „	1° 57'	1° 55'

Now as the azimuth of sunrise varies with the declination, its extreme place at the solstice will of course vary with secular changes of declination, just as its rising at other times of year varies with the diurnal variation; and as the obliquity of the ecliptic is decreasing, and has been so for all historic time, it follows that the sun at the solstice has risen at a greater azimuth, or more easterly than now; and will rise at a less azimuth, or more westerly.

Which of the above nine azimuths of the structure is intended to agree with which of the three solar azimuths? There are thus twenty-seven modes of connection; further, the three solar azimuths are continuously in motion, and will each in the course of ages agree to each of the nine structural azimuths; beside casual small changes, by fluctuations of horizontal refraction, caused by heat or pressure, easily making 2' or 3' change of azimuth of apparent rising.

As the sun's azimuth of rising is decreasing, we may reject all structural azimuths less than that of the beginning of the present rising; and further, as Stonehenge is certainly over 1000 years old, we may reject all azimuths up to 19' farther east, i. e. all less than $1° 23'$, which was the azimuth of beginning of rising at that time. Thus five azimuths are entirely cut out of consideration; those of all the axes, and the north side of the Heel stone: and as the north side is certainly of no importance, it cannot be supposed that the south side of the stone (far below the horizon) should be of importance, when it has a remarkably peaked top, which is unlike that of any other stone there, and which gives a definite horizon azimuth. Is, then, the peak to be observed from the middle of the entrance, or from the slit between the middle trilithon? First, the entrance is 50 inches wide, and its middle is not easily settled without measurement; whereas the slit between the trilithon was only 13 inches wide, about the same as the peak of the Heel stone, the estimated middle of which would give a good definite azimuth on a length of 3400 inches. Next, the horizon is invisible at the entrance, the peak of the Heel rising far above it; and it is only on retreating up the slight rise, to behind the middle trilithon, that the horizon is seen on the level of the peak, by an eye at a fair height of 65 inches from the ground; behind the circle the peak is seen below the horizon. From both these reasons, it seems nearly certain that the point of observation was intended to be from behind the trilithon, to the peak of the Heel stone; as any place between the entrance and the trilithon shares the disadvantages of the former.

There can also be no doubt that the first appearance, and not the middle or completion

of sunrise, was to be observed, as only the first appearance could coincide with the Heel stone at any possible epoch of erection.

The question then narrows itself to the epoch of the azimuth of sunrise being at 1° 24′; this is equal to 9′ change of declination from the present; and hence the sun rose over the peak of the Heel stone at 730 A.D. The probable error of this direction may be taken as about 2′ from all causes; and the observed azimuths of sunrise may easily vary 3′, by a change of 15° Fah. and ½ inch barometer, and—considering permanent climatic changes— 1½′ might be taken as a probable error. Thus a change of 3½′ of azimuth would be about the probable error, and this would equal 1½′ of declination, or about 200 years of time. So the final result, by the theory of sunrise observations, is limited to

$$730 \text{ A.D.} \pm 200 \text{ years,}$$

or perhaps as early as 400 A.D., considering climatic changes.

And at 100 B.C. the sun would rise east of the peak of the Heel stone 16′, or about its own radius, an amount probably quite perceptible to the builders, considering the accuracy with which important parts of the work are laid out.

The large numbers of people that keep up with much energy the custom of seeing the sun rise at midsummer, somewhat suggests that it is an old tradition; and hence that it has some weight, independent of the mere coincidence.

The two other stones on the earth circle, 91 and 93, cannot have any connection with the solstitial risings or settings, as has been asserted.

---

8. Sequence shown by Construction.

From the mean circles shown on Plate I., and their centres, there are important deductions to be made. The centre of the earth circle differs from the three stone circles very much more than they vary among themselves; and the difference (3 feet) is far larger than even the mean error of the circle, much more the probable error. Hence it is not likely that the stone circles were constructed at the same time as the earth; as, if so, the same centre would have been retained; and the earth cannot be later, as it is too good a circle not to have been struck on clear ground. Next, looking at the stone circles' centres, we see they are clearly different one from the other; this also suggests that this part of the work was not done all at once. Which preceded, the bluestone or sarsen? By this evidence, certainly the sarsen, as its error is but small;

whereas the outer bluestone circle has a large error, suggestive of being struck irregularly, after the trilithons were placed. The inner bluestones emphasise this, as nothing could come in the way in striking their semicircle, and they are accordingly as accurate in proportion as the sarsens.

We thus see by the centres that the bluestones were probably later than the sarsens; and as they never were a complete circle, shown by their pairing, it seems very probable that they were added at various times. The great want of uniformity (especially in the outer ones), some short, some long, some rounded ; some flat, some squared ; some shaped at the top, some naturally rough ; some syenite, some schistose, some hornstone ; all shows that they were executed at different times.

On examining the stones and mounds 91 to 94 on the earth bank in a similar manner, it will be seen that they are exactly opposite, stone to stone, and mound to mound. This strongly shows that they are contemporaneous ; as is also shown by the fact that the diameters joining their centres cross each other at $45° 4' \pm$ about $6'$, or just half a right angle ; and further, the diameters are complementary to each other, being symmetrical about the axis of the structure, or at least about an axis differing only $18'$ from the avenue. This shows also that the circle was divided into sixteenths, or $22\frac{1}{2}°$, as each diameter is $\frac{1}{16}$ from the right angles to the axis, or $\frac{3}{16}$ from the axis.

Further, the diameters both pass closer to the sarsen centre than to the earth circle centre (see Plate I.) ; the stones' diameter being one and a half times, and the mounds' diameter two and a half times, as far from the latter as from the former. This altogether implies, (1) that they were very carefully placed ; (2) that there were probably not any other stones, certainly not a circle ; (3) that the mounds and stones on the bank are contemporaneous, as matching in their position ; (4) that they are certainly not earlier than the earth circle, or perhaps the avenue (as Hoare and others have supposed), and are probably not earlier than the sarsen circle. The small pits in the middle of each mound look much as if they had been ransacked when barrow digging was rife in the middle ages ; and this would account for Hoare finding nothing in 92, and bones alone in 94.

We may observe that the earth circle appears to have been complete, and the avenue appended to it afterwards, judging by the arrangement of their junction.

Hence the concluded relative ages of the various parts are as follows : (1) Earth circle. (2) Avenue. (3) Sarsen circle, trilithons, mounds 92 and 94, and outlying stones, more or less contemporaneous. (4) Bluestones.

9. Sequence shown by Measures.

In 'Inductive Metrology' the principles of ascertaining whether a unit of measure was used in the construction of a building, and if so, what length the unit was, have been fully stated; and the methods there used may be applied here without further explanation. As we have seen that the different portions of the work are probably of different dates, it is necessary to treat them all separately. On carefully comparing measurements of all the sarsens, especially of the most completely worked parts, it seems that no unit of measure was used in shaping them. But though the workers might very likely shirk adding so greatly to the trouble of squaring them, by also reducing them all to fixed sizes; yet this would not show that they might not attend to measurement, in placing them, where no great extra labour was required.

Taking the earth circle first, as giving more measurements for inter-comparison, the bank appears to have been equal in width to the ditch, reckoning on a small amount of spreading of the edges; thus the unaltered distance of the centres of bank and ditch apart gives the best indication of their width. This is 225 ± 4 inches. Now the crest of a bank, or the bottom of a ditch, is the least likely point to be metrical; the inner edge of the bank, the neutral point between it and the ditch, and the outer edge of the ditch, are the most likely points to be fixed in laying out the work on the ground. These three are respectively 3595, 4045, and 4495 inches diameter, allowing slightly for spread of edges. Applying then the 225-inch basis of the bank and ditch obtained above, we find these are 16, 18, and 20 of the unit, or radii of 8, 9, and 10, numbers very likely to occur. Taking $4046 \div 18$ as practically the best defined, we obtain $224 \cdot 8$; but the most accurate result will be from the intermediate point, of 17 units diameter, on the crest of the bank; this is 3820 ± 2, $\div 17 = 224 \cdot 70 \pm \cdot 12$. Next, how far is this applicable to other parts? The tumuli centres 92 and 94 are about 3391 apart, and the inner faces of the stones 91 and 93 estimated at 3376 (originally); the latter is better than the tumuli by far, and $\div 15 = 225 \cdot 1$. Further, the radii of these tumuli are 218 ± 5, and 222 ± 6 inches. Considering the difficulty of estimating their ill-defined edges, this is very close to the unit, and the latter (94), which has a ditch, and is thus best defined, is the nearest to it.

On trying the sarsen circle neither the inner nor outer diameter agrees to this unit, and the trilithons and inner bluestones are equally intractable. The outer bluestones, which

may be anything between 900 and 920 diameter, owing to the curved faces of the stones, are closely 4 of these units. The avenue measures seem as intractable as the sarsens. On trying the parallel banks they agree, their length east of the avenue centre being 13,570 inches, which ÷ 60 = 226·2; and west of the avenue 6800 inches, which ÷ 30 = 226·7. This agreement may be only casual, if there is any other evidence against it, as the breadths of the banks apart do not at all agree to this unit. On following westwards, to the portion in continuation of the same line, we find this 11,190 inches long, which ÷ 50 = 223·8. This brings us to the barrows, which are certainly ancient. It has been already mentioned that they are in a very nearly straight line, which suggests some accuracy. The distances of the centres apart are, from the second to the third, just double of that from the first to the second, which equals the distance of the third to the fourth. This length, thus thrice repeated, is 2262 ± 10 inches, and this is 10 of the unit found before in the earth circle. The diameters of the mounds are also closely 5 of this unit, but accuracy is impossible owing to their spreading. Taking up now the sarsens and inner bluestones, the outer sarsens are 1167·9 ± ·7 diameter, and the inner bluestones 472·7 ± ·5 inches diameter; these quantities are very nearly as 10 : 4. The former has been recognised as 100 Roman feet, the latter is therefore 40 feet.* The foot by this would be 11·72, or 11·68 by the sarsens alone. The arrangement of the trilithons is obscure; each of the pairs have their inner faces in a straight line, but there is no scheme sufficiently consistent and distinct to be worth entering on here.

To sum up, there are two units shown. One in the earth circle and its mounds and stones (91–94), and also in the line of barrows, and perhaps the parallel banks. This is, by the best elements, 224·8 ± ·1 inches, excluding the barrows, which give 226·7. In 'Inductive Metrology' I have shown that there is evidence, from entirely different materials, for a prehistoric mean unit of 22·51 ± ·02 inches, probably of Phœnician origin. The close agreement of this with 10 × 22·48 ± ·01 is striking. The other unit, the foot of 11·68 or 11·72, is as closely accordant with the Roman foot, which, though 11·64 in Rome, had a mean value of 11·68 ± ·01 in Greece, Africa, and England. Not that this shows Stonehenge to be post-Roman, as the unit was the great Etrurian and Cyclopean unit, originally derived from Egypt, and it may have been introduced at any date into Britain.

* This rather differs from the statements in 'Inductive Metrology,' as I had not so fully examined the details, and was fettered with the idea of the whole structure being of one epoch, in those statements.

10. Objects found.

It seems desirable to give a brief classified summary, mainly from Hoare, of all the objects found at Stonehenge. These are as follows :—Horns of stags and oxen, rotten bones of men or stags (Duke of Buckingham, 1620)[*] ; heads of oxen, and other animal bones (Stukeley) ; parts of head and horns of deer, and other animals (Hoare) ; fragments of stags' horns under No. 95, bones alone in 94 (Hoare). Cover of incense cup, at 3 feet deep near trilithon (Inigo Jones) ; fragments of Roman and coarse British pottery (Hoare) ; coarse half-baked pottery at 6 feet deep by altar, and in ditch ; bit of fine black Roman pot in hole of 57–58 trilithon ; Roman pot at 3 feet deep by altar (Cunnington) ; Roman tile and mortar (Dr. Parkes). Charcoal, 6 feet deep by altar, and in ditch (Cunnington) ; by altar (Duke of Buckingham, 1620). Batterdashes, heads of arrows, armour eaten out by rust (of iron ?) (Duke of Buckingham) ; large barbed iron arrow-head (Hoare). Plate of tin, with unknown letters, found under Henry VIII. (might this possibly be turned up now in some obscure collection ?). Bactrian coin of 200 A.D., " found by a countryman at Stone-henge " (Southampton Museum).

11. Summary of Evidences on pre-Roman Age.[*]

Besides dividing these evidences into pre- and post-Roman, some in each class are also applicable to a mixed origin, partly of each period.

By the details of the centerings we have seen that there are probably three main epochs in the work ; those of the earth, sarsen, and bluestone circles ; by their differences of centres they probably were arranged at some considerable intervals of time, and this almost precludes a post-Roman origin for the whole, as the Britons certainly had not a century of undisturbed possession after Hengest's slaughter.

The evidence of the measures shows two periods : that of the earth circle and barrows on the 22·5 inch unit, which is probably of Phœnician origin ; and a second period, of the sarsens and inner bluestones, in which a different unit of 11·7 was used. The outer blue-stones fitting to the 22·5 unit is not a coincidence of much weight, as they are so irregular,

[*] The place in Camden's print, dated 1575, where " men's bones are dug up," is outside the trench behind No. 27 : but the trench is drawn so close to the stones, that the spot is not really farther than the tumulus 94. It might possibly refer to the group of barrows out behind No. 19.

and the diameter is so uncertain; this also showing that they were not so likely to be metrical; thus the evidence of their centering outweighs this. This variety in the units points to a protracted erection, and the identity of the earlier unit with that of the group of barrows only containing bronze, glass, and bone, is of similar effect.

The care with which details are executed, especially the exactitude of erecting the stones; the great labour and time required to cut the blocks into shape; and the large quantity removed in surface work, in working the flat faces, and the flat ends and tenons; all these points are evidence of the length of time during which the work was carried on; and, with the signs of incompletion already mentioned, suggest that it occupied considerable time, and was at last dropped for want of materials or interest. The irregular distribution of the pairs of bluestones, and their diverse shapes, is another sign of gradual and irregular addition. All these points, like the first mentioned, are against a post-Roman origin.

An evidence of the pre-barrow age of the avenue, long ago noticed, is the gap in the line of barrows in the direction of the east branch of the avenue. Another token of this is in the parallel banks; these are certainly later than the avenue, by their crossing over it, and yet they run over a barrow and its ditch without effacing it, as if respecting the barrow; suggesting that the barrow was not worthless when they were made; also the western part is very nearly symmetrical about the barrow, as if it was arranged on purpose. These banks are worth more notice, unless they can be clearly shown to be recent, against which there are the reasons already mentioned. The highest objects found in these barrows are bronze spear-heads (2), a bodkin, and glass and amber beads.

Another proof of pre-barrow date, is the occurrence of chips of bluestone in the west barrow of the group west of Stonehenge, accompanied by a bronze spear-head and pin; and chips of both sarsen and bluestone in the bell barrow east of Stonehenge. With regard to the evidences connected with barrows, though very possibly some of them may be of Saxon date, like those in Kent and elsewhere, yet in none of those on which the arguments specially hinge has any iron been found; whereas iron continually occurs in Saxon barrows.

Another evidence brought forward is the collection of the barrows near Stonehenge; and this has been met by a counter-assertion, that the barrows are clearly not arranged about Stonehenge. Both are true, for though none of the barrows are grouped with any reference to it, yet they are thick in the neighbourhood, but not thickest close to Stonehenge,

E

nor placed in sight of it. For on the Ordnance Map (filling some small groups by detailed plans) there are

Within ½ mile	17 barrows = 22	per square mile.
½ to 1 „	89 „ = 38	„
1 to 1½ „	92 „ = 23	„
1½ to 2 „	66 „ = 12	„
2 to 3 „	74 „ = 4˙7	„
3 to 5 „	87 „ = 1˙7	„

But it must be remembered that barrows are seldom or never grouped together, around a central one, or in any regular way; except a straight line, in a few cases. Hence they would not be likely to be arranged about Stonehenge in any case, though they ought to be thickest close to it, if they did refer to it.

The road running past Stonehenge points to a pre-Roman date. The details are given in "Notes on Roads," in the 'Archæological Journal,' 1878, which may be summarised thus:—The road cutting across the avenue askew, close to the circle, is certainly later than the structure, and made when it was disregarded. This road is an important highroad from Andover to Heytesbury, and on to Bristol, and it makes three sharp bends to avoid the great camp at Amesbury, instead of gently sweeping round it, the two portions on either side being in a continuous line. These bends show that it originally ran over the hill and was diverted by the camp. On this bent portion Amesbury has sprung up. This strongly shows that it is an old British road, like many now used (its slightly curved course is just of the character of such), and that it was altered probably at the Roman occupation, certainly not much later, as Amesbury (probably a pre-Saxon town) was built on its changed course. This points to a long pre-Roman date for the original course, and to a more remote time for Stonehenge itself. It has been objected that the present road is only a surveyor's arrangement of the end of the last century. But (beside the fact that Amesbury and Andover must always have had a communication westwards) it is shown in exactly the present course on the earliest road maps, of Seale (1748) and Kitchin (1747). Stukeley's drawings of 1723 also show a road, but close behind Stonehenge; this position is a mistake, as there is no trace of any road visible behind, only a faint single pair of ruts, such as might be made in a few days by a cart running up to the adjacent farm. Those who know how strongly old highroads are scored into the downs, especially up a valley-side (and Stukeley makes this to be a very distinct

highroad in his drawings), will see that it is impossible for any other line for this important road to have been in use near the present course, as there is no trace remaining even on the sloping ground to the east.

One important evidence is the total absence of all inscription, or even a cross; the signs on the lintel, No. 156, being a forgery of 1827. Now there is nothing to show that the Cornish were more civilised than the Romano-Britons; yet in Cornwall there are stones with well-cut Latin inscriptions, of about the same post-Roman date as has been assigned to Stonehenge; or of a century or two later, when they were less, rather than more civilised. And the bluestones, if brought from Cornwall, would be obtained from people well used to lapidary inscriptions.

A similar evidence, though shadowy, is that of the plate of tin, found under Henry VIII. This was inscribed with characters which no antiquary of that age could read. If these had been Roman letters (which were used by the Romano-Britons in Cornwall), or any derivative of them, it would have been intelligible; hence it would seem to have been in an Ogham, Runic, or Eastern alphabet, and in such a locality, probably, pre-Roman.

The weathering of the stones has been considerable, apart from artificial damage; the imposts, 152 and 154, are grooved out to 10 inches deep, and though these may be exceptionally soft, yet others show much change. But on the top of 60, which has certainly been exposed for over three centuries (see Camden's view), and perhaps much longer, there is scarcely any perceptible change, though the rain would lie on it, and favour disintegration. Certainly the cut surfaces of other stones seem, by their appearance, to have been exposed more than five times as long as No. 60.

An incidental point is that Stonehenge, by its tenons and mortises, is an evident imitation of wooden architecture; and as such, is more likely to belong to pre-Roman times, when wood was probably more used, than after the extensive stone and tile buildings of the Romans.

---

12. Summary of Evidences on Post-Roman Age.

The principal evidence for the post-Roman age is that of the Chroniclers, and this is so important that, although often discussed already, a brief summary of them seems requisite.

E 2

28

Though the modern horror of myths has led to the rejection of much of their history, because tainted with the fabulous; yet, besides accidental mistakes, we must draw a wide line between embellishments of true actions, and pure inventions. Most moderns are addicted to the former, though few may be guilty of the latter.*

The two detailed authorities are Nennius (circ. 850), and Geoffrey of Monmouth (circ. 1140), who professedly wrote from a certain Celtic MS. chronicle; Giraldus (1187) alludes to the same facts. They agree that about 462 A.D. the Britons and Saxons, after drawing a treaty, met at Amesbury for its ratification, and that the former were treacherously massacred: Nennius adding that there was a feast, and that the slaughter took place when the Britons were intoxicated; this is extremely probable, as nothing would be more likely than a feast on such an occasion, and the Saxons would wish for it (and are said to have proposed it) in order to begin the attack at better advantage. The convent where they met was "in the mountain of Ambrius." Now Stonehenge is on tolerably plain ground, and there is no likelihood of buildings having existed there, but by far the most likely place for a monastery would be on the steep hill just over Amesbury, known as Vespasian's Camp,† which probably contained perfect buildings of Roman period at that date. Next, after the slaughter, they were buried in a burying place near the monastery—observe, not at the monastery; and Aurelius erected the monument on the spot where they were buried. These points are quite consistent, a feast would not be held out in open country, but in a town. They met then for a ratification festival, in some buildings on Vespasian's Camp; there the Saxons massacred the Britons, and the latter were carried out to the spot then known as a burying place, *near* Amesbury, and there interred. And on this spot Aurelius. Ambrosius afterwards erected a monument.

Now an incidental invention is seldom carried out and referred to in incidental allusions

---

* Eponymic derivations are considered fatal objections to historic veracity, and Isaac Taylor boldly says, "When we read in the Saxon Chronicle that Portsmouth derives its name from a Saxon chieftain of the name of Port, who landed there, we conclude at once that the name of Port is *eponymic;* or, in other words, that no such personage ever existed." Yet our nobility have their usual names from places. If this canon is held by future historians, and if some writer makes the jumble that Wellington and Melbourne in England, as well as at the Antipodes, are called after those premiers, our modern history will be credited as little as the Chroniclers are now. What is more natural t ian that the surname by which a barbaric invader was known should be the name of the place he first occupied? And it is a venial mistake to invert the order of derivation. The historical existence of Wihtgar (to take Taylor's other case) need not be doubted from his name, any more than the existence and deeds of the nobles known as Suf*folk* and Nor*folk* in later history. Latham says of these cases, "The names of Port and Wihtgar give us the *strongest* facts in favour of the suggested hypothesis, viz. the *ex post facto* evolution of personal names out of local ones."

† Only a name of Stukeley's.

in subsequent accounts, whereas this is thrice mentioned again. The previous account is in book vi. chap. 15, and viii. 12 of Geoffrey. In viii. 16, Aurelius is said to be buried near the convent of Ambrius, within the Giant's Dance. In viii. 24, Uther Pendragon was buried close by Aurelius; and again, in xi. 4, Constantine was buried close to Uther, in Stonehenge. All this is very consistent in general, and also in the detailed difference of "near" and "within" also, a different expression is used in each case, which does not look like repeating a conventional formula, or copying from one entry to another.

Another allegation against the historical character of the narrative is the interference of Merlin. But though his life (or their lives) are embellished elsewhere, in this incident there is nothing of which a modern contractor need be ashamed. He is only said to have used "the engines that were necessary" to remove the stones in Ireland to the ships, and they were brought over in the most matter-of-fact manner. Giraldus similarly says that by aid of his engines he took down the stones with incredible ease to bring them over for the erection of Stonehenge.

In short, in these accounts there is no discrepancy, and nothing to tax our credulity; and if other evidences should indicate that, by a very natural aggrandisement, the whole was ascribed to the authors of a portion, it is a fault that has often occurred in later writers, and which modifies, but not destroys, their testimony.

The other literary references are: (1) The circular temple of Apollo, mentioned by Hecatæus, which, if referring to Britain, might apply to any of the megalithic circles. (2) The Welsh triads, which, if genuine, need not in this case be pre-Roman. (3) Cuhelyn (circ. 550) says that the meeting of the Saxons and Britons "was in the precinct of Iôr, in the fair quadrangular area of the great sanctuary of the dominion." The epithet quadrangular is very irreconcilable. Hoare connects it with the cursus, but it seems inapplicable. Does it refer to square buildings in Vespasian's Camp, or to the camp itself, to which we have just seen the chronicles seem to point, and which might be reckoned in one property with Stonehenge? (4) Aneurin (circ. 550) mentions the "stone cell of the sacred fire," and the "great stone fence of the common sanctuary," which last seems very applicable to Stonehenge. One most important point in these last evidences is the attention they show to have been bestowed on megalithic remains in post-Roman times, which renders the more likely their erection or amplification at that period.

The frequent finds of Roman pottery are not conclusive, as they may have been

dropped accidentally after the erection. The pieces found at 3 feet deep by the altar, and the piece of tile raked out by a gamekeeper from a hole *under* one of the stones, and obtained by the late Dr. Parkes, as I am informed, are the most satisfactory. Careful and intelligent digging is much needed to settle this. The diameter being 100 Roman feet has been already mentioned to be no proof of age, as this unit was used for the early Cyclopean buildings of Greece and Italy.

The finds of iron are important. Hoare's arrow-head may be of late date, lost accidentally; but the armour found in 1620, from being eaten through with rust, must almost certainly have been of iron, especially as Celtic bronze armour is unknown, and this almost proves post-Roman burial. What especially emphasises these finds of iron, is, that no bronze is recorded to have ever been found there, and if wholly or mainly belonging to a bronze-using people bronze ought to be more frequent than iron.

The assumed low state of the pre-Roman inhabitants has been adduced as a proof that they could not have erected Stonehenge. But their state has been much exaggerated; or rather what was written of a few has been applied to all. A thick population, accustomed to agriculture and trade, using metallic currency, and familiar with working in metals, appears to have occupied the southern counties. The abundance of field-terraces, on ground which does not now pay for cultivation, all over Salisbury Plain and other barren downs, corroborates the statements of the Roman writers.

The evidence of the arrangement of the barrows has been fully entered on in the previous pages.

It has been said that the builders destroyed two barrows in making the earth circle, which must therefore be of a much later age; but the connection of these barrows with the circle has been here shown to be intentional.

The evidence from the azimuth of midsummer sunrise has also been fully stated, and shown to point to a post-Roman date; and, if the solar reference be granted, the pre-Roman date would require us to suppose that the builders disregarded an error of at least half the diameter of the sun, which is unlikely.

The negative evidence, that no mention of Stonehenge or other such monuments is found in Roman writers, is worth very little, considering the remarkable omissions that occur in the most careful of the ancient topographers and historians.

31

13. Summary of Evidences on the Use.

By the examination of the details of the construction we have seen that the various parts are of different dates, and may therefore possibly be of different intention. The various theories propounded are either, (1) Sepulchral, (2) Memorial, (3) Religious, or (4) Astronomical; or combinations of some or all of these.

The Sepulchral may be taken as a certain element at some period, considering the instances of human bones reported in the sixteenth and seventeenth centuries, that the two tumuli are posterior to the earth bank, that Hoare found bones in one of them, and that Geoffrey repeatedly mentions burials. The name of the stone 96, called the Friar's Heel, with the absurd story of a heel mark in it, may have arisen from its being called the Heel stone, from Anglo-Saxon *hélan*, to hide or conceal, just as a cromlech at Portisham, Dorset, is called the Hel-stone. This would be probably from its covering a burial, as heal, hell, hele, all refer to horizontal covering. If it was used also for a vertical covering it might refer to its hiding the rising sun, as seen from the entrance.

The Religious intention is strongly contradicted by the absence of all traces of fire or calcination on the so-called "Altar stone," and by its very low position, almost flush with the ground; if any altar was there it can hardly be supposed (from its site) not to be this stone, which is, nevertheless, so unlikely. Another objection that has been raised is the assumed absence of wood at early dates. But Webb, in 1665, says (p. 188, ed. 1725) that from Amesbury to Stonehenge was a forest full of great trees, until two centuries before his time. This is not at all impossible, considering the flourishing woods that now exist on the chalk downs; and if some care be at present necessary to aid them in some cases, climatic changes might easily favour them more in former times, especially as a whole country being covered would affect the rainfall, and facilitate the growth of wood by checking the side pressure of wind. The absence of irregularity in the ground from the decay of large roots is, however, much against it. The lack of any carving on the stones is somewhat against a religious intention, as most religions have symbols; but it is no proof of hasty erection, as a hundred times the trouble requisite for it has been spent in shaping the stones. The repeated finds of stags' horns would seem to point to sacrifices or else to feasts, and confirm the statement of a forest having existed there.

The Astronomical theory has the strong evidence of the very close pointing to the midsummer sunrise, but apparently none other that will bear scientific scrutiny.

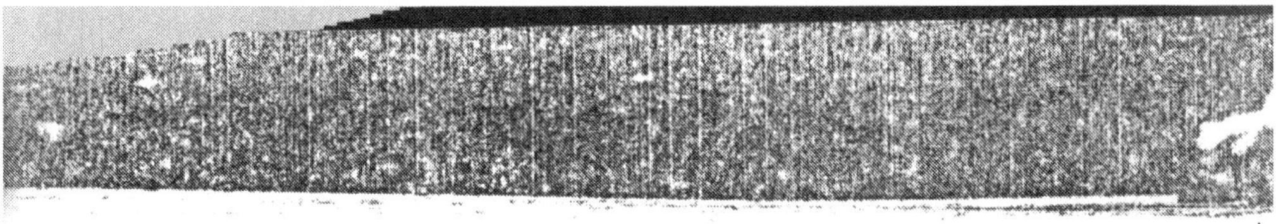

32

14. Concluding Remarks.

Having now stated all the facts and arguments, as far as I know them, I may be asked "What is your conclusion?" I can only answer by giving due weight to each of the arguments somewhat as follows, and as no two persons will weight them alike, my readers must each weight them for their own satisfaction, as they may see fit.

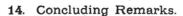

	Pre-Roman date. Pro.	Con.	Mixed date. Pro.	Con.	Post-Roman date. Pro.	Con.
Different dates, by centering	4	..	4	..	..	4
Different dates, by measures	3	..	3	..	..	3
Long in erection, by work	2	..	2	..	..	2
Gap in barrows for avenue	1	..	1	..	..	1
Barrows before banks	1	..	1	..	..	1
Chips in barrows	2	..	..	2	..	2
Road cutting avenue	4	..	3	1	..	4
Absence of inscription	4	..	..	4	..	4
Plate of tin	1	..	1	..	..	1
Weathering of stones	4	..	4	..	..	4
Chroniclers	..	8	6	2	8	..
Roman pottery	..	2	..	2	2	..
Iron objects, no bronze	..	3	..	3	3	..
Midsummer sunrise	..	4	4	..	4	..
No Roman account	..	1	..	1	1	..
Totals of weights, pro and con.	26	18	29	15	18	26

The weighting is done by considering what arguments would balance each other, and how far two or three poorer ones would balance a better. From this the preponderance is only 3 in 5 in favour of a pre-Roman, and against a post-Roman, date. A mixed date, some parts pre- and some post-Roman, satisfies the arguments somewhat better, reconciling 2 in 3 of them. This accordingly seems to be the most probable, and the least unlikely history of it would be :—1st. The earth circle made, like many other plain earth circles of great regularity in other places, for religious, sepulchral, or civil purposes. 2nd. The avenue added to it, pointing roughly to the sunrise. 3rd. Interments in the circle, in mounds, and under stones; the sarsen trilithons and circle gradually erected; the Heel stone placed to fix sunrise more accurately, when the trilithon was put up. 4th. The flat stone 95, and the altar stone 80, placed as tombstones over interments, carelessly, and

somewhat askew. The neighbouring groups of barrows partly before and partly after this date; and interments at various dates in Stonehenge, because it was known as a burying place at the next epoch. 5th. In post-Roman times, the Britons massacred at Amesbury, and buried in Stonehenge. The uniform set of inner bluestones brought from Ireland by Merlin's skill, and erected in memory of them. 6th. Aurelius Ambrosius, Uther, and Constantine, and probably other chiefs, buried at intervals in Stonehenge; the rougher outer bluestones, which are of various characters and shapes, probably of various dates, and show less care and ability, erected to their memory. This outline, as a whole, seems to reconcile the various arguments more than any other; but I only regard it as the least unlikely supposition.

What is now necessary, to settle this much-disputed subject, is careful digging. By having a timber frame to carry the weight of a stone, clamped by its middle, it would be possible to remove the whole of the disturbed soil in layers from underneath each of the still erect stones, leaving the stone suspended; the earth being replaced and rammed, the stone would undergo no perceptible change, and could not be upset during the operation. The details of the work have been sketched out, and the whole frame would only cost a few pounds.

Another work, very urgently needed, is securing the great trilithon upright, 56, which now leans so much. This stone, from the evidence of various drawings, has inclined farther and farther since its first tip in 1620. In 1660 it was at 75°, in 1720 at 70°, in 1870 66°, and it is rapidly going over farther at present. On its fall, which cannot be far distant if unsecured, it will certainly break across, as it is cut unusually thin, has a large flaw in the middle, and will fall across its fallen lintel. To save this stone, the largest native hewn stone in England, and next to Cleopatra's needle in size, will be far better worth while than attempting to re-erect the fallen trilithon, which undertaking was mooted some years ago. It should be simply screwed and pulled back, rather askew, until it is upright, as this will probably restore it to its original place better than any other method. If some similar attention was given to a few of the outer circle stones that seem in peril at present, it would not be misplaced.

Many of the facts (particularly those of structural details), and half of the arguments, are here published for the first time; and the various references to the publication of the other facts and theories mentioned here, have not been given in detail, as the object was the

F

structure, and not the history of its literature, which may be found in the pages of Inigo Jones, Dr. Charleton, John Webb, Stukeley, John Wood, John Smith, Sir R. C. Hoare, Dr. Fergusson, the Wilts Nat. Hist. Mag., and the Proceedings of the Archæological Societies. So much fresh evidence has appeared, on carefully examining the errors of construction, that it seemed requisite to embody it in a complete statement of all the arguments, especially as such a collection has not hitherto been published.

My best hope is that the arguments here brought forward and collected, will soon be rendered obsolete by a thorough investigation ; though probably the plan will never be superseded by one of greater general accuracy, though perhaps small corrections may be made in it, as in all fallible work.

LONDON : PRINTED BY EDWARD STANFORD, 55 CHARING CROSS, S.W.

The plan of Stonehenge is only one of a series of considerably over a hundred surveys of earthworks and stone remains. It is proposed to publish selections of these at intervals, if there should prove to be a sufficient interest in them to defray their production. The most important, such as Chun Castle and village, Dawnsmaen, Boscawenoon, and other circles, Buttern Hill circle, Addington Stones, Fripsbury, Amphrey's Rings, Barbury, the Bishop's and All-Canning's Works, Steeple Langford, &c., would be taken first. Probably sections containing half-a-dozen plans, each of half a page of this size, and correct to about $\frac{1}{200}$ of an inch, with brief letterpress, would be the best arrangement. Any suggestions on this subject may be addressed to the author, Bromley, Kent.

The figures of the ground-levels on Plate II. not having printed clearly, they are here re-stated; all above the bench-mark on the Friar's Heel.

	Inches.
At 350 inches behind No. 16	60·5
450 „ „ No. 54	53·7
150 „ „ Nos. 52–3	60·0
Mid between stone and earth circle, behind No. 52	31·5
Mid between stone and earth circle, behind No. 3	24·7
Mid between stone and earth circle, behind No. 29	32·3
700 inches behind No. 25 ..	44·1
Mid between stone and earth circle, behind No. 23	58·5
100 inches behind No. 57 ..	68·5
Between Nos. 48 and 29	63·7
„ Nos. 32 and 3	43·3
„ Nos. 70 and 59 a	56·8
Lowest point of middle, 130 N.E. of altar ..	46·3

Middle of upper side of altar stone, 80	60·0
Mean level of tops of circle stones	213·3
Mean level of tops of circle lintels	241·7

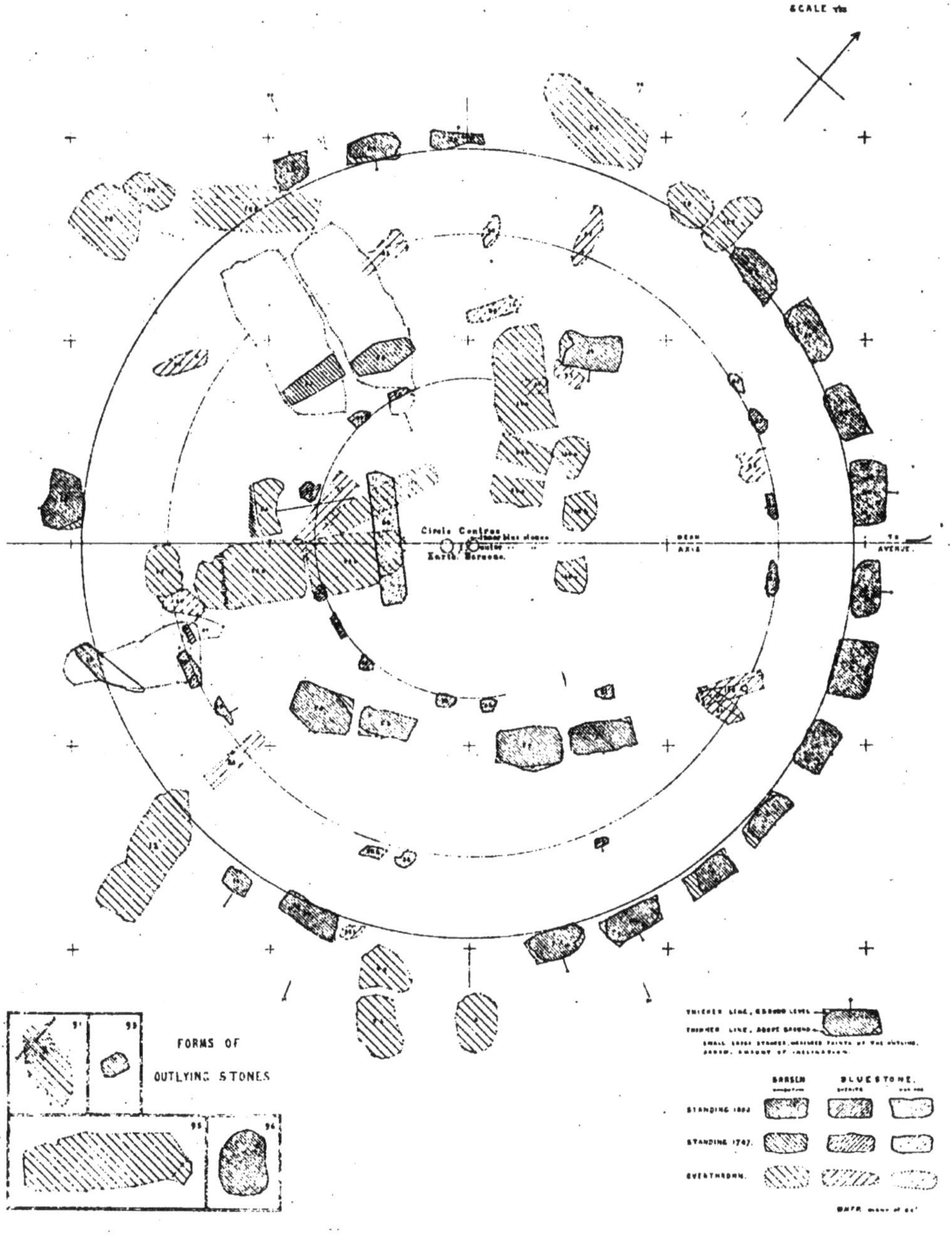
SCALE
Circle Centres
Earth Barrows
AVENUE
FORMS OF
OUTLYING STONES
THICKER LINE, GROUND LEVEL
THINNER LINE, ABOVE GROUND
SARSEN
BLUESTONE.
STANDING 1747.
OVERTHROWN.

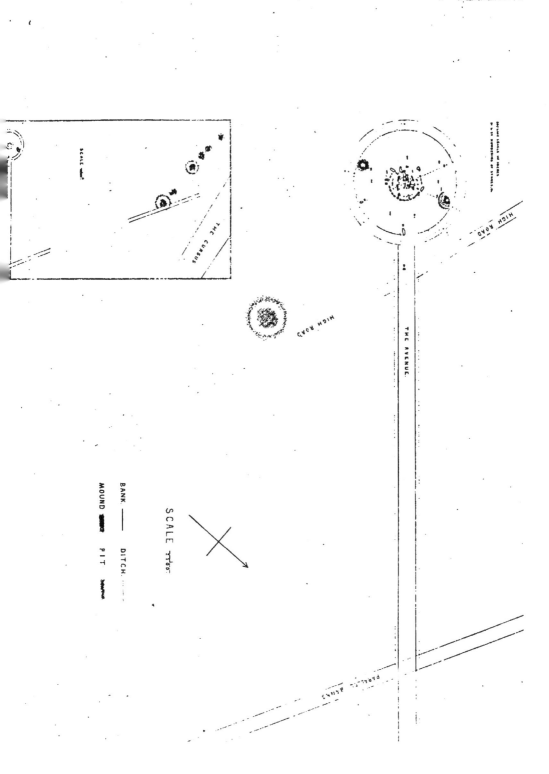

SCALE

BANK —— DITCH ……
MOUND ▰▰▰ PIT ▰▰▰

THE CURSUS

HIGH ROAD

THE AVENUE

HIGH ROAD

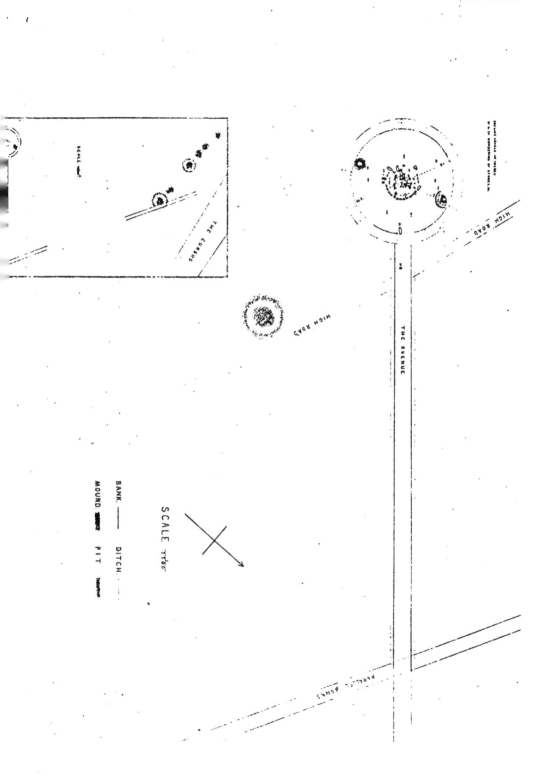

SCALE

BANK. ——— DITCH. · · · · · ·
MOUND. ▬▬▬▬ PIT ▬▬

THE AVENUE

HIGH ROAD

HIGH ROAD

THE CURSUS

SCALE

BARROW BUSHES

Lightning Source UK Ltd.
Milton Keynes UK
UKHW020639190722
406066UK00005B/727

9 781376 297959